MEDITATIONS

After the Bear Feast

MEDITATIONS

After the Bear Feast

The Poetic Dialogues of
N. Scott Momaday and Yuri Vaella

Translated and Edited by
Alexander Vashchenko and Claude Clayton Smith

SHANTI ARTS PUBLISHING
BRUNSWICK, MAINE

MEDITATIONS
After the Bear Feast

The Poetic Dialogues of
N. Scott Momaday and Yuri Vaella

Shanti Arts Publishing

Interior and Cover Design by
Shanti Arts Designs

Front cover image: N. Scott Momaday, *Bear*
Photograph by Lana Kiana Garcia
Used with artist's permission

Back cover image: Yuri Vaella and N. Scott Momaday, 1998
Photograph by Alexander Vashchenko

Shanti Arts LLC
193 Hillside Road
Brunswick, Maine 04011
shantiarts.com

Printed in the United States of America

ISBN: 978-1-941830-38-3 (softcover)
ISBN: 978-1-941830-39-0 (digital)

Library of Congress Control Number: 2016943048

To bridge builders and gatekeepers

of the indigenous past, present, and future

There is a sacred essence within us
That is always there, always here.

— N. Scott Momaday

Contents

Image Credits

Bear art, both those that carry titles and those that the editor has elected to identify with a variation number, were graciously made available through the courtesy of N. Scott Momaday and were provided by St. Martin's Griffin from the 1999 edition of *In the Bear's House*. (Images 1, 4, 6, 7, 9, 12, and 15)

Image 1. N. Scott Momaday, *Ancestral Voice.*

Image 2. Alexander Vashchenko dines at Taras Bulba, a Ukrainian restaurant in the heart of Moscow named for the tale by Nikolai Gogol, 2007.

Foreword

Susan Scarberry-Garcia

IN THE SUMMER of 1997 Alexander Vashchenko and I led a cultural excursion to Moscow and Tobolsk, the oldest city in Siberia. Participants included four Navajo and Apache students, a Navajo medicine man, and a videographer from Navajo Preparatory School in New Mexico. Leonid Lar, a Nenets artist, had invited us, along with the noted American Indian author N. Scott Momaday. On this initial native exchange in Siberia, our students danced and sang with Khanty, Mansi, and Nenets youth, who in turn performed throat singing and fishing dances for them in nearby Tyumen, and Momaday became enthralled by the dark shamanic imagery of Lar's paintings in his Tobolsk studio. Earlier, at Moscow State University, Momaday had read from *The Man Made of Words* (St. Martin's, 1997), and the American Indian students sang for the Russian students. At the end of our Siberian visit, Vashchenko arranged a meeting between our group and the Khanty novelist Yeremei Aipin, who screened an Estonian documentary on the Khanty Bear Feast at his home. For Momaday, this film served as a compelling introduction to Khanty ritual. Although he would not meet Yuri Vaella until the following year in Varyogan, the 1997 excursion introduced him to the landscape and cultures of western Siberia, where he found himself at home among the great rivers, sand, evergreens, and bears.

The following summer, at a fish camp on the Ob River in northwestern Siberia, Momaday walked the boggy land with Yuri Vaella, a gifted Native Siberian writer of the forest Nenets people, discussing their mutual interest in indigenous oral traditions. It was a journey Momaday had dreamed of for years. To see the Siberian landscape was to imagine his Kiowa ancestors' ancient routes over tundra, taiga, and water bundled backward 30,000 years. The occasion was a gathering of writers and scholars from three continents in honor of Yeremei Aipin.

At dusk, after a meal of fish head soup, the group gathered for a photograph in the tall grasses before heading back to a small excursion boat. Later, as I sat on board videotaping, Momaday produced a small tape recorder from the pocket of his red windbreaker and leaned closer to Vaella, who was sitting for the interview in a gray jacket that mirrored the overcast sky. Vashchenko sat beside Vaella, providing simultaneous translations in Russian and English, as he had done the year before. Momaday began with the idea that, among American Indians, it is known that animals and humans understand each other, that there is a "network of understanding." Vaella concurred: "Animals and humans are links of the same chain and we can understand each other. This not only involves thinking but also looking at each other; the eyes are part of the understanding." Later, after describing his experiences as a moose hunter, Vaella spoke of his work as a reindeer breeder. "Bear is the natural enemy of Deer, [so] man, as host of the Deer, makes a pact that Bear will not harm his Deer; in return, he won't harm him." Vaella paused and gazed thoughtfully at the river. "Bear can understand whatever a human tells him," and if Bear were to

violate the pact, then "the beast would feel ashamed." Vaella and
Momaday — whose Kiowa namesake animal is the Bear — were
speaking the same language.

The poetic dialogues that follow are a record of the first
acquaintance between poets from American Indian and Native
Siberian cultures as they came together to recognize their
astonishingly similar cultures and parallel reverence for the
natural world. Beginning with their meeting on taiga ground,
Momaday and Vaella exchanged poems for more than a
decade — a mutual inquiry into the power of place, the nature of
healing, and the arc of eternity. With the invaluable assistance of
Alexander Vashchenko, a mutual friend, colleague, and translator,
they discussed their shared values concerning the kinship of
humans and animals, and the critical transmission of traditional
knowledge in the contemporary world. *MEDITATIONS After
the Bear Feast* opens up a transcontinental poetic conversation
between indigenous writers who are at last able to directly
communicate with one another.

IN 2000 VASHCHENKO, Momaday, and I participated in a
village conference in Agan, Siberia, hosted and organized by
Yeremei Aipin, but it was not until 2004 that Momaday would
see Vaella again, at a conference on Finno-Ugric literature in
Khanty-Mansiysk. Delegates from half a dozen nations attended,
including Khanty poet Maria Vagatova and American scholar
Andrew Wiget, who has spent more than twenty years among
the Siberian indigenous peoples. Momaday read his poetry
and Vaella screened a film about traditional lifeways and the
education of his grandchildren on their native grounds. Once

again Vashchenko provided the translations, and participants enjoyed a deep-minded exchange amid the gifts of books and traditional dolls. During these journeys in Siberia, Momaday was hosted in villages and towns, on remote native grounds and waterways, and developed an abiding attachment to the land and people along the Ob River. As these contacts increased, Alexander Vashchenko gathered, translated, and edited — along with Claude Clayton Smith, who had hosted him and Aipin at Ohio Northern University — *The Way of Kinship: An Anthology of Native Siberian Literature* (University of Minnesota, 2010). This remarkable volume is the first to present the diverse wealth of Native Siberian literature to a world that has largely been closed off from access to its rich oral and written traditions. With a Foreword by Momaday and representative work by Vaella, Aipin, Vagatova, and nine other Native Siberian writers and artists, *The Way of Kinship* has engendered a keen interest among native North Americans in the parallel aesthetic expressions of culture and spirit.

IN 2010 I co-organized "Threads of Kinship: Dialogues with Native Siberian Writers," a weeklong event held at the Institute of American Indian Arts (IAIA) in Santa Fe, New Mexico. Here, Momaday, along with Native American writers Sherwin Bitsui (Diné), d.g. nanouk okpip (Inupiat-Inuit), Evelina Lucero (Isleta, Owingeh Pueblos), and James Stevens (Akewesane Mohawk), interacted with Vaella, Vagatova, Aipin, and his daughter Marina who came from Russia with Alexander Vashchenko. Over the course of roundtables and readings, which included Claude Clayton Smith and Andrew Wiget, Vaella and Momaday renewed their close friendship and listened to new poetry. The visitors attended classes and encouraged students to develop their own storytelling voices. As of this writing, years later, students still remember Vaella — in his green hooded tunic — concerned about the reindeer calves about to be born on his native grounds back in Siberia.

Reflecting on his experience at IAIA, Vaella said, "Scott [Momaday] felt for me like an immediate relative living in a neighboring *choom* [tipi]. This is the kind of kinship that we have found in our languages together." Asked about the significance of the IAIA gathering, he replied: "As this natural native world broadens from the local place outward, to the entire country and other peoples across oceans, the sense of relationship broadens, too. People can see that they are not alone, but rather members of a wider circle."

Destiny seemed to draw Momaday and Vaella together, or was it fate from a deeper source? As Momaday wrote of his early years in *The Names: A Memoir* (Harper & Row, 1976): "I was much alone. I had no brothers or sisters, and . . . my peers were at removes from me, across cultures and languages. I had to create my society in my mind. . . . My features [as a child] belied the character of my ancient ethnic origin. There are early photographs of me which might have been made thirty thousand years ago on the Bering Strait land bridge." Thus, when Momaday found Vaella, his bear brother, he expanded a branch of his own family tree, and reaffirmed that he had never been truly alone in the world.

The poetic dialogues of Momaday and Vaella are a journey in themselves, and as Momaday observes, "There are many journeys in the one." Within the poems a narrative emerges about searching for paths to sacred places where the poets, in either human or bear form, can meet to sing and dance in the wilderness. During this journey there are moments of great solemnity, from Momaday's highly ritualistic opening poem "Summons," in which the speaker implores the universe to find a shamanic bear doctor for him, to Vaella's closing poem, "My Grandmother's Values," in which the speaker exhorts:

Let all of our songs
From the Bear Feast
Resound forever.

Always there is a calling to the powers of creation to bless the paths that the poets have chosen and to restore the universe through the beauty of words.

Image 3. N. Scott Momaday with the Russian-English edition of *MEDITATIONS After the Bear Feast* presented by Andrew Wiget at the Zane Bennett Gallery in Santa Fe, New Mexico, in 2013.

Image 4. N. Scott Momaday, *Bear, Variation 1.*

Always There, Always Here

Alexander Vashchenko

I N THE ENTIRE history of world literature little has been written about poetic dialogues per se. They are a rare and special genre. The poetic dialogues presented here are unprecedented; there is nothing analogous to them. The unique exchange is based on a kinship of traditional cultures vastly removed from one another in terms of geography, habitat, civilizations, and ways of life. Once they had met, the two participants, a North American Indian and a native Nenets of western Siberia, wished to continue their intimate conversation in verse. The result was two poets responding to each other in harmonious voices in order to express their most vital thoughts and feelings.

N. Scott Momaday, poet, prose writer, essayist, dramaturg, and graphic artist, who was awarded the United States National Medal of Arts in 2007, is descended from the nomadic tribe of the Kiowa Indians, warriors and hunters of the bison, who once so bravely defended their lands against the onslaught of the U.S. army and endless waves of white settlers. Momaday was the first among his fellows to gain fame as an American Indian writer. For some time, no one in the United States understood the implications of this. In general "Indians" had been written off into oblivion because of books like *The Last of the Mohicans* (1826) by James Fenimore Cooper. But N. Scott Momaday became the founder of *modern* [editor's italics] American Indian literature. In his novel *House Made of Dawn* (St. Martin's, 1968), which won the Pulitzer Prize in 1969, Momaday disclosed the deep problems of contemporary Indians, illustrated the fundamental differences between the value systems of Indian culture and American individualism, and expressed pride in his heritage and confidence in its future.

The capacity to keenly experience the beauty and sacrament of existence, which demands a no less amazing sacrament of language, inevitably led Momaday to the path of poetry. Like his prose, his lyrics demonstrate a wide range of influences. The American classicists Dickinson, Frost, and Winters are present, as well as the Indian oral tradition: the voice of the nomads of the plains and the farming tribes of the American southwest, and especially the "prophetic" songs and warrior songs. Images evoking aboriginal magic, combined with the special melodies and rhythms of poetic speech, enchant readers and draw them into the sacred act of the inspired word.

Momaday's creative road has been long and fruitful, lasting more than four decades. In the author's name are the novels *House Made of Dawn* (Harper & Row, 1968) and *The Ancient Child* (Doubleday, 1989); the frequently anthologized extended story "The Way to Rainy Mountain;" plays, memoirs, essays, and of course, poetry. Momaday's career path changed directions dramatically in 1974, when he was sent as the first Fulbright scholar to teach a half-year term at Moscow State University. During this time he devoted his leisure to seeking out museums, where he began to sketch and draw. As he would one day categorically state: "It's in Russia that I had my start as a graphic artist."

Image 5. Yuri Vaella visits the pueblo of Jemez, New Mexico, in 2010, while at the Institute of American Indian Arts in Santa Fe for "Threads of Kinship: Dialogues with Native Siberian Writers."

Eventually, Momaday was able to actualize his lifelong dream of visiting Siberia. By that time a small book of selected works by Yeremei Aipin, *I Listen to the Earth* (Ohio Northern University, 1995), which I had translated, had come out in the United States, thanks to the efforts of my friend and colleague Claude Clayton Smith, who edited and polished the text. Reading the chapter dedicated to the Bear Feast, Momaday could already sense in himself the impetus for a poetic dialogue. A few years hence, poems dedicated to Aipin and Yuri Vaella, whom Momaday had met in 1998, appeared in his book *In the Bear's House* (St. Martin's Press, 1999). Its very title — *In the Bear's House* — evokes the Bear Feast, and the Siberia / Bear theme occurs three times within the book's structure. Momaday's Indian name (*Tsoai-talee*) occurs in a myth in which a boy is turned into a bear; it is also the name of a number of Kiowa chieftains.

The other participant in these dialogues, Yuri Vaella, was born Yuri Kilevich Aivaseda in Varyogan in west Siberia in 1948. Vaella is a reindeer breeder who spends most of his time in his ancestral deer camp. He is of the taiga Nenets people and takes his pseudonym, Vaella, from an ancient taiga Nenets clan. During the Civil War of 1918 – 19, the Nenets moved south to the Agan River and adopted the culture of the Khanty "reindeer people." Vaella's first teacher was his grandmother, who introduced him to the oral tradition. As a teenager Vaella spent a number of years in a boarding school and then went into the army, where he worked as a carpenter. In the 1980s he studied creative writing at Moscow State University. He began to publish in 1988, writing poetry, short stories, and prose sketches in both Nenets and Russian. He is the head of the Association of Private Reindeer Owners, and his stand against the Russian oil industry's invasion of his native grounds has always been strident.

In 1989 he organized the first picket line among Khanty hunters to protest the blatant encroachment of the oil barons. In Varyogan he established the Museum of Traditional Culture of the Taiga People. In addition to writing and publishing folktales, poems, and essays, Vaella has made oral recordings of folktales. His volume of collected poems, *White Cries*, was published in Surgut in 1996, followed by four more books of poetry and prose: *Triptychs* (2001), *Speak to Me* (2004), *The Land of Love* (2009), and *Threads of Kinship* (2010).

Vaella's lyrics, light in flight but intense in thought, are widely know in Pirobye, an urban locality in the Khanty-Mansiysk Autonomous District, and beyond the borders of Siberia as well. They have been translated into a number of European and Eastern languages. I myself saw to it that his poems were published in English in a variety of American literary magazines and journals, and included representative samples of both his poetry and prose in *The Way of Kinship*.

Vaella is a genuine master of oral storytelling, and his verbal skill is felt in both his poetry and prose. He writes as if he had lived the life of his heroes, along with their travel companions, their friends, the villagers they meet, and others. Given his acquaintance with Aipin and Momaday, it was no surprise that with the latter, in the poetry of *In the Bear's House,* associated his speaker with the hero of the Bear Feast. In the poetic dialogues that follow it is plain to see how deeply Momaday was impressed by the theme of the bear's self-sacrifice as well as the reverence shown by his kinfolk. His poems carry the penetrating cry of loneliness and the thirst for union with mankind.

The main theme that rings out in the poetic dialogues of Vaella and Momaday is stated in the final two lines of Momaday's last poem, when he declares that the sacred essence within us is "always

27

there" (that is, in the people's past), "always here" (in that these values will remained unchanged and unchangeable).

The dialogues begin with a summons from Momaday:

The Poetic Dialogues of N. Scott Momaday and Yuri Vaella

SUMMONS

— for Yuri Vaella, from N. Scott Momaday
Moscow, 1998

Where is the bear doctor? Where is he?
I have come from the north, and I thirst.
I have come from the east, I hunger.
I have come from the south, I am tired.
I have come from the west in great need.
Where is the bear doctor? Where is he?
In my life I have known the bad things.
In my life I have known the good things.
I have come from the dusk, and I dance.
I have come from my home to go forth.
Where is the bear doctor? Where is he?
Who will outfit me for my journey?

Influenced by accounts of the Bear Feast and the ceremonial paraphernalia he had seen in Tobolsk in 1997, Momaday began "Summons" in 1998 on the train ride to Siberia, where he met Vaella, dedicating his poem to him upon returning to Moscow. They met again in Siberia in 2004 and in Santa Fe in 2010, where Vaella issued the reply below. In the exchanges thus begun, a meditative, dramatic mood characterizes Momaday's poems, whereas Vaella's optimistic responses call for a living participation in the flow of events. Vaella's answer to "Summons" was in just such a spirit:

HERE I COME

*— for N. Scott Momaday, from Yuri Vaella,
Siberia, 2010*

And here I come!
I await you on your path.
In my entire life I have no closer brother.
In my entire life no better companion.
We can compare our strides.
We can exchange our growls.
We can cross our stares.
May our path never narrow.
And here I come!
We shall enter the circle of your kinsmen.
We shall cross the lines of my kinsmen.
On which side will we find a harsh word?
On which side will we find a kind word?

Please summon your children, no bigger than pinecones.
I'll summon my children, no bigger than birch leaves.
May the children step lightly and play.
May the children dance in the spirit of freedom.
I've never met anyone who suffers from words as I do.
Never met anyone like you, who weeps in song.
In your lifetime, if you've ever heard a harsh word,
Forget it! In your lifetime, if your soul ever felt pain,
Forget it! It was to test your sense for true words.
So here I come!
I await you on your path.
Do you think I'm the one who restores your soul?
In truth, you restore mine!

Vaella's poetic structure and style contain a precise echo of Momaday's tone, while the contents reveal a kinship of spirit and a system of values with an intimate desire to encourage and share them both. From here on, a recognition and evocation of an ethical / aesthetic kinship (family, animals, a shared path, a circle of kinfolk, children, words, songs) becomes a basic theme of the dialogues. In the process, the poems are conscious of both sides; the participants feel as if generations of relatives are standing beside them. And it is for their sakes, and for the sake of the future, that the dialogues will continue.

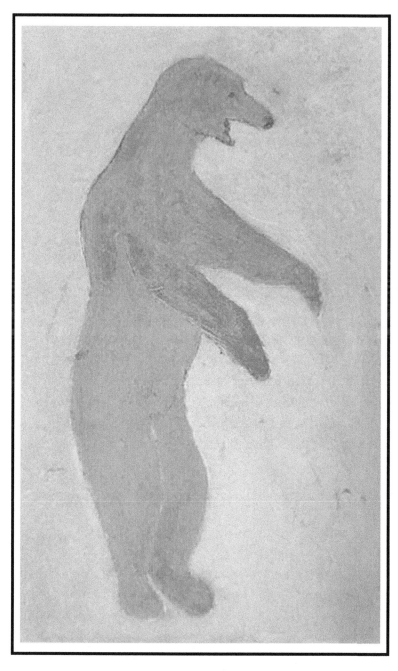

Image 6. N. Scott Momaday, *Standing Bear*.

IN THE FOREST

—for my brother, Yuri Vaella
USA, 2012

Oh my brother, I hear your footsteps
In the forest. They are strong and even;
They sound the rhythm of your great heart.
You go among the tracks of the bear.
Always the bear will guide you.
You will come to an open space among the trees.
And there you will dance. You will sing the songs
Of the elders, those who have made sacred the earth.
I hear your footsteps and your songs.
Oh my brother, I will dance with you.
Together we will celebrate our bear being.
We will keep alive the holy fires.
Aiyee!

The conversation here progresses in terms of near kinship. Momaday uses "brother," a word for which Vaella, below, selects a more telling Nenets synonym, *Nyame-e.* In the Nenets language the word for the elder brother is *Ytya*, but the more intimate and common word is *Nyame-e — Nya*, for short — the elder or younger brother, cousin, partner, or person of spiritual closeness. Through Vaella's influence, Nenets' intonational and oral-poetic turns make their way into Momaday's style, rendering his images more concrete in contrast to the abstract symbolism that is often characteristic of his work.

Vaella's response becomes a series of good wishes for the future, growing out of a union of two kindred hearts, able, through time and distance, to feel the shared rhythm of their beating:

Let It Be So

— these words are for N. Scott Momaday, my Nya
Siberia, 2012

Aiyee! — Truly,
This was the way it was:
I thought the forest deafened all sound.
But you heard my footsteps.
I tried to tread lightly
Among the tracks of the beasts.
But you — Oh my Nya! —
You felt the vibrations of my heart.
You heard my footsteps
In the ancient songs of the Elders.
You caught the echo of my heart,
Though I tried to hush its beating
Within the intricate Bear Dance.

Let our children sing through the centuries,
As many as pinecones.

Let our grandsons dance through the centuries,
As many as birch leaves!
Let them gather around the sacred hearths.
May they be happy with the songs, stories and
Legends that we send them through time;
And those we won't live to pass on —
Let them imagine themselves . . .

Those who are to sing —
Let them sing freely!
Those who are to dance —
Let them dance joyfully!
Those who are to play in the dramas
And sketches and sacred rituals —
Let them play creatively!
This is the way it always was
And should be in the future!
Let them celebrate our own Bear essence!
Let them bring their offerings
Into the Sacred Forest,
Generous offerings
Like the wishes in prayers!
Let them put on the masks
And strike the drums in unison!

Let the beasts on the animal path
Always descend from Higher Ground.
And may our descendants, with sharpened arrows,
Await them warily.
Aiyee! Oh my Nya!
Let it be so.

Image 7. N. Scott Momaday, *Bear, Variation 2.*

Now Momaday strikes out in a new direction:

THE TRACKS

— for Yuri Vaella
USA, 2012

My true brother,
I have heard a strange story:
A man came to the night ceremony.
He was dressed in rich garments,
Fine pelts and beautiful ornaments.
He stood at the edge of the grounds
And made no sound.
No word, no song rose from his mouth.
No one knew this man.
But all knew he was powerful,
That he had great medicine about him.
When the ceremony was ended he was gone.
The people went to the edge of the grounds
To see where his tracks might lead.
But there were no human tracks;
There were only the tracks of a bear.

O my brother,
Were the tracks yours?
Did you come to the ceremony
Bringing the deep wild spirit of the forest with you?

Did you make holy the night
And draw the stars closer to the earth?
Will you forever be remembered
In your beautiful fur coat and ornaments?

I long to walk with you in the taiga.
We will make deep tracks in the snow,
And we will tell the old holy stories,
And we will sing the sacred songs.

Here, the bear becomes an important intercultural factor, giving birth to trust and to a depth of understanding between the participants of the dialogue. The bear is an indispensable intermediary between kin, who by chance were separated by thousands of miles, but He powerfully overcomes the distance. In truth, the bear is our most ancient kinsman. The story is told in France that in the Lascaux caves, famed for their illustrations done by primitive peoples, a visitor was somehow drawn into an older cave where tourists are not taken. There on the floor, next to each other, lay two skeletons — one of a man and one of a bear. Only here, the man's legs had been attached to the legs of the bear, and the bear's legs to those of the man.

In this third poetic dialogue both participants feel themselves to be in the place of the bear, out of necessity taking it upon themselves to imagine what this is like — to be at once both spirit and sacrifice. Unfortunately, dramatic circumstances intruded into the further development of the exchanges between Momaday and Vaella. Momaday was suffering from diabetes. At

Image 8. Susan Scarberry-Garcia, Alexander Vashchenko, Claude Clayton Smith, and Yeremei Aipin *[left to right]* enjoy a meal at the Aipin family fish camp while on a boat excursion along the Ob River in 2003.

the conference in Santa Fe he was forced to read his new poems from an armchair on rollers. Later, Yuri Vaella, underwent an operation on his lungs, followed by problems at a nomad camp. In the drought-stricken summer of 2012, his living quarters burned up with his belongings. Regardless of these setbacks, the poetic dialogue eventually resumed.

A Prophetic Dream

— for N. Scott Momaday, from the Nijnevartovsk oncology ward
Siberia, April – May 2012

You, oh my Nya, have asked me:
Was I there
At that sacred place?

Well, I had a dream
Last night.
I was descending from the Earth's back
In the form of a Bear,
So my hide might stir
After hibernation,
So I might awaken,
Feel agile, enlivened!
It appears that I was hungry,
It appears that I'd lost my strength,
It appears that Life itself
Was ebbing from my body . . .

I found nothing to eat on the taiga.
I had no strength to butcher
Even the most feeble yearling
That fell behind
Among the reindeer
In my own herd . . .
And as I passed among the people
I heard voices all around:

"Will you eat this?
Will you eat that?
Will you . . . ?"
But as I looked closer
At their outstretched hands
There was nothing to eat!
In the hands of some —
Gold pieces for trade.
In the hands of others —
Bundles of cloth for making clothes.
In yet other hands —
Pretty shawls to adorn
The heads of women.
From all of this,
In my hunger,
What could I eat?
What need did I, the
Bear,
Have of such things?
Can it be
That they mistook me
For a deity?

And the eldest of them
Said to me:
"You once were a human,
But now you've taken the form of a beast.
You once lived among us,
Now you come from the taiga.
Is it better to live separate lives?"

Of course not.
It's not better for me to live separate from you.

But you've learned to feed yourselves
From the hand of the State.
You no longer fish for yourselves.
No longer hunt for yourselves
Or pasture your reindeer.
And in return for your love
The State's agents pour
Gold pieces into your pockets.
Is that why you're so blind?
I myself don't like gold.
It turns my stomach . . .

And the eldest one spoke again:
"Let's jump over this little fire here.
If you do, you'll be human again."
So I looked at the campfire —
And the campfire blazed up!
It was a raging furnace!
And we,
Gathered around the sacred fire,
Were ready for the sacrifice.
But we wanted to ask the gods
For one more happy day —
So that the skis of the youth
Would glide freely over the snow,
And ask of the gods
A second favorable day

So that the youth would walk
With squeaking heels in the snow.
We would ask of the gods
A third favorable day
So that their women would live
Till their hair grew as white as snow,
And their daughters would live
To wean their children . . .

So, gathering speed, I decided
To jump over the fire,
Because it occurred to me:
"What if I'm the one to be sacrificed?"
But someone held me back.
I remember clearly — I tried hard
To jump over the fire,
But someone very strong
Pressed my shoulders down,
Wouldn't let me take off,
Angering me,
Screaming in my ear:
"What are you doing?
You're ruining the hospital's dishes!
Wake up! Wake up before you
Hurt yourself!"
And as I looked around with sleepy eyes,
I realized I was in a hospital ward,
Trying to jump over the bedside table,
With its kitchenware and medical
Instruments, as the night nurse and

Doctor held me down,
Trying to quiet me
To restrain me,
To make me obey.

And today,
As I looked myself over —
Oh! What's this?
The hem of my shirt is burnt!
The cuffs of my pants are burnt!
When did that happen?
After all, in a hospital ward
There's no open fire . . .
And now you, oh my Nya, ask me,
Was I at that sacred fire,
Where our relatives — mine and yours —
Spoke with the gods?
I know for sure:
In my dream I was there!
But why are my clothes
Burnt for real?

In this, the longest poem of the dialogues, Vaella brings together many poignant themes. The dialogues as a whole are linked by the theme of sacred insight, and in the poem at hand it becomes the main focus. The delirium experienced by the speaker in the hospital becomes a prophetic dream: the tribal folk walk still farther from the revered works of their grandfathers, while the change in values comes at a cost. From the point of view of the Bear, the speaker takes on modernity, confronting us with the question: where is the meaning of life to be found? It is, after all, the poet's nature to strive for the unknown, to go beyond the limits, in spite of reality. And so the hospital doctor — who is generally performing his duty — simultaneously represents those who would like to "restrain" the poet, to "quiet" him, to make him "obey."

Finally, there is present here the profound readiness of the poet / prophet to sacrifice himself, if this is what is required for his people's survival.

As if sensing that these unique exchanges were coming to an end, Momaday wrote:

A LETTER TO YURI VAELLA

— USA, 2013

In the twilight
Among the forest spirits
I find you, and an old recognition
Comes upon us. We are met
In a greeting of love and respect.
You are my son, and I am yours.
We feast upon the stories of our lives
And dance in the tracks of the bear.
We sing of heroes and of gods
Who have bequeathed us courage and hope.
You are my brother, and I am yours.

We know the mysteries of the taiga,
The rivers and the marshes
In which the animals are emissaries
And bring us dreams of other worlds.
You are my father and I am yours.
We are of the same ancient blood
And the bones of our ancestors.
You are my grandfather, and I am yours
We glory in the words of origin,
The prayers of Creation and well-being.
There is a sacred essence within us
That is always there, always here.

Vaella replied with:

My Grandmother's Values

—for my Nya
reindeer camp at Tiui-Tyakh, February 2013

Once
My grandmother told me,
"When starting upon a long journey
Take these everlasting values with you:
do not cheat,
do not steal,

do not harm anyone,
do not kill,
do not deny help to the weak,
do not let anyone offend your neighbor,
do not violate your clan's customs,
do not desecrate anyone's shrines,
and after returning from your journey,
pay respect to your Father and Mother!"

Your words, oh my Nya,
Remind me of my grandmother's words.
They may remind others of sacred things, too.
Because in today's world
True values
Are often confused with the false . . .

Please become a wise grandfather for me,
So I may be a clever grandson.
Please become a strong father for me,
So I may be your true follower.
Please become a keen brother for me,
So I may have a partner in all ventures.
Please become an elder son for me,
So my soul will know what to tell you.
Please become a young grandson to me,
So I can simply take you by the hand.
Please become a great-grandson to me,
So I may continue in you.

Let the blessed world continue —
The sun, the wind, the tundra, the deer!
And let all of our songs
From the Bear Feast
Resound forever.

And of all of our songs,
Let those first sung at the Bear Feast
Resound forever.

The pair of poems that concludes the dialogues followed after a year's hiatus. Nonetheless, the shared feelings of the preceding revelations have united the participants powerfully. Thus a tone of finality is apparent in the last poem, a final summing-up. Henceforth, perhaps the practitioners of both literary traditions — the Indian and that of the indigenous peoples of Siberia — will sense their closeness more strongly and continue to develop with a greater sense of fellowship. The main theme, in the form of an overarching conclusion, rings out in the last line of Momaday's poem, when he states that the sacred essence within us is "always there" (that is, in the people's past), "always here" (that is, these values will remain unchanged and, one would like to add, unchangeable).

The dialogues of *MEDITATIONS After the Bear Feast* are remarkable in and of themselves; they contain a mutual recognition of kinsmen across oceans and seas, across centuries of mutual isolation. They are likewise remarkable in their profound naturalness, sincerity, and internal freedom. Perhaps the chief value of this poetic evocation, however, is the declaration of fundamental

Image 9. N. Scott Momaday, *Bear, Variation 3*.

human values, delineated clearly and in detail, expressing the authors' deepest aspirations as spokesmen for traditional cultures. It is also remarkable that there is no single point of disagreement; instead, Momaday and Vaella share a deep concern for the fate of the world.

This poetic calling forth offers an important lesson to all of us who live from day to day, with confused priorities, without a thought to eternity; who miss the point; who subordinate ourselves to false standards; who forsake our original nature — our distant, ancient kinsman, the Bear, that mighty spirit of Mother Nature and powerful symbol of our enormous, universal nation. He who, as before, hopes to unite us all.

Image 10. Bear prepared for the Bear Feast.

In The Bear's House

A Note on the Bear Feast

Andrew Wiget

V ERY DEEP IN Chauvet Cave, France, in one of its biggest chambers, the massive skull of a cave bear was recently discovered on top of a flat-surfaced rock. In this ancient gallery, where human hands painted wondrous dreams on torch-lit walls, it is unlikely that the skull simply fell into place. The relationship between bears and humans is at the core of some of the oldest forms of cultural activity, traceable to the late Paleolithic "cultural revolution," which marked the introduction of art and ritual into human history. Today, in the cave of our dreams, we redraw images from those caves of stone.

In *In the Bear's House*, through a series of dramatic dialogues between Urset, the prototypical bear, and Yahweh, the proper name of God in the Old Testament, N. Scott Momaday seeks to understand the nature and significance of the bear as an incarnation of his — and our—spiritual longing. "Bear," he writes, "is the keeper and manifestation of wildness. Something in me hungers for wild mountains and rivers and plains. I love to be on Bear's ground, to listen for that old guttural music under his breath, to know only that He is near. And Bear is welcome in my dreams, for in that cave of sleep I am at home to Bear."

The bear's claim as deity and totemic ancestor is much more than metaphorical. For many non-agricultural peoples the bear, the "animal that walks like a man," is the principal symbol through which the human community has articulated its relationship to the world. Across the boreal forests of the circumpolar North, a widespread Bear Cult acknowledges and honors the bear as ritual ancestor and Master of the Forest. While the bear is an important personage in the religions of many tribal peoples, the most elaborated and highly developed forms of the Bear Cult are found in western Siberia, where the Bear Feast represents the most ancient layer of their culture. This is especially true for the Khanty, among whom Yuri Vaella's Forest Nenets people settled and, like Vaella, found spouses.

For the Khanty, the Bear Feast (*pupi kot*, "the bear's house" in Khanty) is part of a larger complex of Khanty belief and custom concerning the role of the bear as Lord of the Forest and his special relationship with humans. Khanty believe that all bears are the responsibility of Pupit Kon, the Lord of the Bears, who is one of the sons of the high god, Numi-Torum. When Pupit Kon was living in the sky-world as a human, he looked through a hole in the ground and saw far below him this present world, the forest covering it like a fine fabric. He pleaded to be let down into this world, and Torum obliged, lowering him in a cradle at the end of a chain, some say made of iron. He was instructed not to harm people, raid the cache in tree houses where their food was stored, or disturb their graves. The bear was also to carry out the will of Torum in executing justice, and for this reason the most solemn oath a Khanty can take is to swear, often in the presence of a bear's head, that if the truth is not

Image 11. This tree marks the site of a bear sacrifice among the Khanty. The temperature was -30° F in 2011 when this photograph was taken in a sacred grove at Torum Maa, a Khanty hilltop open-air museum established by Yeremei Aipin.

being told, the bear should destroy him. In the Surgut region, bears' skulls are preserved, and the head of the bear that has been given a Bear Feast is often preserved in Khanty homes in an honored place — sometimes next to a Russian icon — and made the subject of regular veneration, addressed in prayer and offered money and fabrics.

Typically, a Bear Feast is a consequence of a special hunt organized for the purpose of gathering the community to honor the bear, and the occasion is becoming increasingly rare. Such ritual hunting is always done in winter by a group of men, who find a bear's den, wake the bear from sleep, and drive it out of its den to be killed. The manner in which it is skinned in the field suggests an undressing of a person. The hunting party then forms a procession, singing songs honoring the slain, undressed "Old Man," as the bear is called out of respect. As with Yahweh, the bear's name is ineffable, and the Khanty employ a special language of elaborate epithets. When the bear is killed, the hunters must mark a tree with the sign of the bear, which is the top view of the bear's head flanked by paws. Adjacent to it they cut slashes indicating the number of men in the hunting party. Nearing the village, they announce their arrival by firing guns, and the people of the village come out to greet them with a song about bringing the bear, the honored guest, into the village. The bear is never brought into the house through the door, but through a smoke hole, window, or similar opening. Then the indoor festival begins, continuing with similar songs and rituals, four days for a female bear, five for a male.

The Siberian honoring of the bear touched N. Scott Momaday profoundly, in part because, as has already been noted, Momaday's Kiowa name, from the Kiowa oral tradition, refers to a bear, a given name that Momaday cherishes as an intuition of himself. When he first met Yuri Vaella in 1998, Momaday found a kindred spirit, another who personally understood the spiritual necessity of the bear. What he wrote in *In the Bear's House* might well describe the great discovery of their first meeting: "There are people in the world who would not wish to be in the world, were not Bear there as well. These are people who understand that there is no wilderness without him. Bear is the keeper and manifestation of wilderness. As it recedes, he recedes. As its edges are trampled and burned, so is the sacred matter of his heart diminished."

We are all Bear clan; we are all kin.

Adapted by the author from his book: Andrew Wiget and Olga Balalaeva. *Khanty, People of the Taiga: Surviving the Twentieth Century.* University of Alaska Press, 2010.

Image 12. N. Scott Momaday, *Bear, Variation 4*

The Heaviness of Silence

Andrew Wiget

WHEN ALEXANDER VASHCHENKO passed away on June 11, 2013, after a short but terrible battle with cancer, we lost a professional colleague of international stature who had become an essential part of the ongoing conversation in the humanities between Russia and North America. I, and undoubtedly many others, lost a best friend.

Nearly thirty years have passed since I first met Alexander Vashchenko in the summer of 1985. The study of Native American literature was then only an emergent phenomenon in the United States, when I learned that a visiting scholar was going to speak on that topic at the University of Pennsylvania. I heard an intense, bookish-looking fellow present a very good reading, both sensitive and informed, of Momaday's *House Made of Dawn*. In 1989 I invited this man to tour the Southwest with me, and the following year he invited me to the Soviet Union. We spent the month of August together, as he took me all over Russia, from Karelia in the far north to the Caucasus in the south. In trains and planes, cars and boats, we talked and talked, days and nights, telling stories and jokes, sharing personal experiences, our sense of our own country and each other's, discussing literature and teaching and writing. By then, I had learned to call him Sasha, the affectionate nickname for Alexander.

At that time Sasha was working in Moscow at the Gorky Institute of World Literature of the National Academy of Sciences, contributing articles on Native American literature, canonical authors — and later Chicano authors — to what would eventually be a new five-volume history of American literature, definitive for the USSR. Later he would proudly show me the fifth and final volume, pointing out that he had contributed articles on Native American writers to every one. When I mentioned that I would like to speak with anyone who had been working with Siberian native peoples — because I understood that their stories and traditions bore some similarity to those of American Indians — Sasha introduced me to one of the Gorky folklore scholars just returned from a Siberian expedition, Olga Balalaeva, who would later become not only my colleague but my spouse. Together the three of us organized a 1992 international expedition to the Siberian Khanty, the first of many trips to Siberia for Sasha and me. A year later, Sasha brought out a two-volume Russian-language collection that he edited called *In Nature's Heartbeat.* One volume represented his selection of Native Siberian writers, the other his Russian translations of Native American writers. This remarkably ambitious, even visionary project anticipated by twenty years *The Way of Kinship,* the recent anthology of Native Siberian literature in English. Now, of course, we have the present Momaday-Vaella poetic dialogues.

In 1994 Sasha published a translation of *Black Elk Speaks,* and later his translations of Momaday. He was an indefatigable and superb translator, supporting any effort that would foster dialogue

Image 13. Andrew Wiget tends to his camera at his
family dacha near Moscow in 2012.

between indigenous literatures. When I shared the news of his death, one Siberian writer remarked despairingly, "Now, who shall we find?" Indeed. At present there is no one else. Sasha had become the indispensable link between two worlds.

A few days before he passed, we talked in the hospital, remembering our times together. I suggested to him that we had been bridges between our countries and cultures. He thought of that metaphor a minute and corrected me: "Gates," he replied. "We were gates." I have since been contemplating the difference between those metaphors. Bridges are permanent constructions, built over time, piece by piece, and there is some truth to that image in our work. But Sasha's image is more in character: gates are points of entrance, doors pushed aside in an act of the will, demanding strenuous effort but finally opened as wide as the widest arms, so crowds can flood in. For me and many others — such as Scott Momaday and Yuri Vaella, and you, the reader — Sasha was such a gate, opening a passage between hearts and worlds that will never close.

On September 12, 2013, just three months and a day after Alexander Vashchenko died, Yuri Vaella was felled by lung cancer, even though he had never smoked. He had just visited our apartment in Moscow in March, which was, strangely enough, the last time Sasha was able to visit our home. His business card read: "Reindeer Herder. Poet." It's not a combination one meets every day; then again, Yuri Vaella was not the kind of man one meets every day. In a time and place where most people claim to have been shaped by their environment, Yuri Vaella, with some truth, could claim the opposite — to have shaped his own life as well as his world.

Vaella's most recent work was these poetic dialogues, meditations on and through the bear, with the Native American (Kiowa) writer, N. Scott Momaday, poetry rooted in yet another friendship brokered by Alexander Vashchenko. Part of the achievement of this poetic dialogue now rests in the heavy silence of the absence of Yuri and Sasha. And from the Bear's House comes a murmured growl of recognition:

Now, who shall we find?

Image 14. *Totem*. This lithograph by Bashkirian artist Rinat Minnebayev
depicts elements of the Bear Feast ceremony shared by Khanty, Mansi,
and Komi peoples who live near the Taiga Nenets in northwest Siberia.
It was inspired by Minnebayev's reading about the Bear Feast.

The Black Bird

N. Scott Momaday

YURI VAELLA WAS my friend — my friend in person, my brother in spirit. He was a man of parts, a holy man, a hunter, a philosopher, and above all a poet. He was at home in the element of language, in his native Taiga of words. He was rich in experience and common sense, in perception and wit. He was an original. I remember well the first time I heard him read from his work; I paraphrase one of his offerings:

> This morning a black bird flew across my window.
> So what?

I was won over. Here was a man from whom to expect the unexpected. Here was a kindred soul.

Yuri and I met several times over the years, both in his native land and in mine. Our friendship grew in the most natural way. We were poets and men of the natural world. He was a Native Siberian and I an American Indian, and although we spoke different languages we each possessed a rich oral tradition. It seemed inevitable that we should construct a dialogue in our respective native voices.

MEDITATIONS After the Bear Feast — a dialogue — is a brief exchange between two native men who are spiritually related to each other and to the sacred earth they inhabit. Taken as a whole, it is also a poem, an ode to Creation and the spirit of the wilderness.

I am simply glad that I had the honor and privilege of knowing Yuri Vaella, that we came together on common ground, and that our meeting is celebrated and made permanent in our voices.

I say to Yuri, "Where is the bear doctor?" and he replies, "On your pathway I am waiting for you."

It is so, my brother, I follow in the tracks of the bear.

These remarks were written for a memorial conference for Yuri Vaella held in Estonia and read there by Andrew Wiget on behalf of N. Scott Momaday. The title, "The Black Bird," is my own, inspired by the following entry from "Vaella's Visit," which records a more serious side of Vaella than the playful comment that struck Momaday:

At sunset a black raven flew by our dwelling up the slope of the mountain, perhaps looking for a place to spend the night. He looked familiar to me. It must be the nestling that was born near our camp on the Tiyi-Tiakh two years ago. Last year, while flying overhead, he sent down his droppings and they hit me on the shoulder. But I understood him quite well — he didn't want to offend me. He just wanted me to remember him better. Since then he often follows me in my wanderings.

— Claude Clayton Smith

Image 15. Alexander Vashchenko waits to translate the words of Yuri Vaella at the "Threads of Kinship" conference, Institute of American Indian Arts, 2010.

Image 16. N. Scott Momaday, *Bear, Variation 5.*

Editor's Note

Claude Clayton Smith

MEDITATIONS AFTER THE BEAR FEAST (A Dialogue) was published as a bilingual (Russian / English) chapbook by Yugrafica Publishing in Mansiysk in 2013. The commentary by Alexander Vashchenko was added in "World of the North," *Mir Severa* (No. 1, 2013), published in Moscow by Slava Ogrysko. The epigraph that introduces this text is inspired by Andrew Wiget's final conversation with Alexander Vashchenko. To the metaphor of bridges and gates I would add the image of a wheel, with Alexander Vashchenko as the hub and those of us who knew him as the spokes, thereby connected to the circle of life, itself a native concept.

I met Alexander Vashchenko in the fall of 1989 at an international Hemingway conference at Ohio Northern University, where one topic under discussion was Indians in the work of Hemingway. The conference director, my friend and colleague Tod Oliver, suggested that an appropriate gift for Vashchenko would be a copy of my book *Quarter-Acre of Heartache* (Pocahontas Press, 1985), which details the successful modern struggle of the late Chief Big Eagle of the Paugussett Indian Nation to prevent the termination of his tribe's tiny reservation by developers in Trumbull, Connecticut. In 1976

Chief Big Eagle, along with Clyde Bellecourt and Russell Means of the American Indian Movement (AIM), physically defended the reservation against local, state, and federal authorities, while noted civil rights attorney William Kunstler saw the case through the courts. I asked Chief Big Eagle to inscribe a copy of the book, and he responded with a lavish and heartfelt message about nations walking in peace. The gift delighted Vashchenko; he stayed up all night reading, and first thing in the morning, as I headed a university van toward Hemingway territory in northern Michigan, said he would like to translate *Quarter-Acre of Heartache* into Russian, to join other Native American narratives in the fifth and final volume of his studies of American literature, the book he would later proudly show to Andrew Wiget. An invitation to Russia for the Chief and me followed, and we made two trips to Moscow and Leningrad, in the summer of 1989 and again in 1990.

On our first visit, following the collapse of the Soviet Union, we met with the Indianists — Russian citizens (including one Native Siberian) who have dedicated their lives to the preservation of Native American culture. On the second we attended the annual All-Union Soviet Indianist Powwow, an event detailed in my book *Red Men in Red Square* (Pocahontas Press, 1995). It seemed no coincidence to anyone that Chief Big Eagle was a member of the Bear Clan.

Vashchenko returned to Ohio Northern University in 1996 with Yeremei Aipin for programs related to the publication of Aipin's chapbook *I Listen to the Earth*, the book that introduced N. Scott Momaday to the Bear Feast. It was the first of my editing and translating adventures with Sasha, which eventually led to the publication of a preliminary edition of *The Way of Kinship* in a special issue of the *North Dakota Quarterly* (2003), followed by the extended edition from the University of Minnesota Press (2010) and "Vaella's Visit" in the *North Dakota Quarterly* (2013). By then I had returned to Russia twice: in 1993 for a conference at the Gorky Institute, and in 2003 with Sasha and Susan Scarberry-Garcia for a joint conference sponsored by Ohio Northern University and Moscow State University: "Surviving by the Word," funded in part by a grant from Exxon-Mobil. (Earlier, the Mobil Oil Corporation had supported the publication of *I Listen to the Earth*.) For *MEDITATIONS After the Bear Feast*, as with our other texts, my job was to polish and edit Sasha's English translations for an American audience.

It was my decision to delay the sad news of the passing of Alexander Vashchenko and Yuri Vaella until the end of these poetic dialogues so that the reader might experience the shock it produced among the writers and scholars who knew them. My friend and colleague James Walter of Ohio Northern University, whom I introduced to Sasha in Moscow in 1993, was kind enough to retranslate his poetic commentary and help with problem lines in Vaella's poems, when the former could not be found among Sasha's papers. Even before the news of their deaths had spread, however, Sasha and Yuri had been memorialized in the following two poems by Nathan Romero (Cochiti Pueblo), a student in creative writing and studio arts at the Institute of American Indian Arts, Santa Fe, New Mexico, who had participated in *Threads of Kinship: Dialogues with Native Siberian Writers* in 2010. By concluding this book with these poems, my intent is to pass the spirit of Alexander Vashchenko and Yuri Vaella — together with the inspiration of N. Scott Momaday — to the next generation of Native American and Native Siberian writers.

Aiyee!

Image 17. Poet and artist Nathan Romero of Cochiti Pueblo discusses his animal drawings with a "Text and Image" class at the Institute of American Indian Arts, Santa Fe, New Mexico, in 2010.

THE BRIDGE

— Nathan Romero

He sat there at every occasion.
He reminded me of something classical,
an enigma in suit and tie.
There was something meaningful in his eyes.
If one were to combine all alphabets, the Ob River,
Rodin's thinker, Russian architecture, snow
and a brave heart, it would equal this man.
He was a scholar who became more and more like us.
What is it to be a bridge between cultures?
What is it to translate timeless words?

What is it to be a bridge?
Many rivers flow through his existence.
He told us that storytellers will save the earth,
And I believed him.

The Reindeer Herder

— *Nathan Romero*

The Tundra to the north has an improbable hero.
In green garments with orange piping and hood.
He stands watch over his herd.
He stands watch over all of us.
The thunder of hooves upon the floor of his wilderness
echoes the rhythm of wonder in our desert —
not one hoof but many, since time was time,
snow mud and stone well traversed.
Across the sanctity of creation and blessed waterways
he awaits the new ones eagerly.
There will be much to do when they arrive.
Make no mistake: they are what he knows.
He is in their consciousness from birth to death.
He is in my memories like moving clouds.
Make no mistake: he will be a constellation one day.
I will look up at the night sky
and tell younger generations:
"There he is — the reindeer herder, the poet, upon his sledge,"
and they will stand in awe.
They will know that he meant something here

Recommended Reading

Aipin, Yeremei. *I Listen to the Earth.* (chapbook of fiction & nonfiction) Translated by Alexander Vashchenko and Claude Clayton Smith. Ada, Ohio: Ohio Northern University, 1995.

Bobrick, Benson. *East of the Sun: The Epic Conquest and Tragic History of Siberia.* New York: Poseidon Press, 1992.

Forsyth, James. *A History of the Peoples of Siberia: Russia's North Asian Colony, 1581-1990.* Cambridge: Cambridge University Press, 1992.

Golovnev, Andrei and Gail Osherenko. *Siberian Survival: The Nenets and Their Story.* Ithaca, New York: Cornell University Press, 1999.

Momaday, N. Scott. *Again the Far Morning.* Albuquerque: University of New Mexico Press, 2011.

_____. *Three Plays.* Norman: University of Oklahoma Press, 2007.

_____. *In the Bear's House.* New York: St. Martin's Griffin, 1999.

_____. *The Man Made of Words.* New York: St. Martin's Griffin, 1997.

Slezkine, Yuri. *Arctic Mirrors: Russia and the Small Peoples of the North.* Ithaca: Cornell University Press, 1996.

The Way of Kinship: An Anthology of Native Siberian Literature. Edited and translated by Alexander Vashchenko and Claude Clayton Smith. Minneapolis: University of Minnesota Press, 2010.

Vaella, Yuri. "A Nomad's Progression to the Sedentary Life". (poem) Translated by Alexander Vashchenko and Claude Clayton Smith. *Transference.* Western Michigan University. Fall 2013.

_____. "Vaella's Visit." (Nonfiction excerpt from *Threads of Kinship*) Edited and translated by Alexander Vashchenko and Claude Clayton Smith. *North Dakota Quarterly.* Spring 2013.

_____. "Song of the Agan Woman." (poem). Translated by Alexander Vashchenko and Claude Clayton Smith. *Ice Floe.* University of Alaska. Summer 2011.

_____. "To the Bear." *Grrrr: A Collection of Poems about Bears.* Sausalito, California: Arctos Press, 2000.

Ziker, John. *Peoples of the Tundra: Northern Siberians in the Post-Communist Transition.* Prospect Heights, Illinois: Waveland Press, 2002.

See also the English-language website of The Russian Association of the Indigenous Peoples of the North (www.raipon.info/en) and the Arctic Council website for organizations of Arctic Peoples (www.arcticpeoples.org).

Acknowledgments

WE ARE GRATEFUL to the editors and their assistants at the University of New Mexico Press, St. Martin's Griffin, *North Dakota Quarterly, Visions International, World of the North,* Yugrafica Publishing, and, of course, Shanti Arts Publishing, who made this book possible.

MEDITATIONS After the Bear Feast (A Dialogue) was published as a bilingual (Russian / English) chapbook by Yugrafica Publishing in Mansiysk, Siberia, in 2013. The commentary by Alexander Vashchenko was added in *World of the North, Mir Severa* (No. 1, 2013), published in Moscow by Slava Ogrysko.

"Summons" and "Here I Come" (under the title "Dialogos") appeared in *Visions International,* Fall 2012. The poem "Summons" is from *In the Bear's House* by N. Scott Momaday. Copyright © 2010 University of New Mexico Press, 2010.

Contributors

N. SCOTT MOMADAY [Kiowa] — Poet, prose writer, essayist, dramaturg, and graphic artist. He was awarded the National Medal of the Arts in 2007 and the Pulitzer Prize in 1969. He is an adjunct professor at the Institute of American Indian Arts in Santa Fe, New Mexico.

YURI VAELLA [Aisaveda] (1948 – 2013)— Reindeer herder, poet and prose writer, and political activist. He was of the Forest Nenets people of western Siberia. His work has been translated into a variety of European and Eastern languages.

ALEXANDER VASHCHENKO [Alexandr Vaschenko] (1947 – 2013) — Scholar and translator. He was senior researcher at the A.M. Gorky Institute of World Literature in Moscow, Russia, and later chair of the Department of Comparative Studies in Literature and Cultures at Moscow State University.

CLAUDE CLAYTON SMITH — Professor Emeritus of English at Ohio Northern University. The author of eight books, he is, with Alexander Vashchenko, editor and translator of *The Way of Kinship* and works by Yuri Vaella and Yeremei Aipin.

SUSAN SCARBERRY-GARCIA — Visiting Scholar of English at the University of New Mexico, Adjunct Professor at the Institute of American Indian Arts, Santa Fe, New Mexico, and the author of *Landmarks of Healings*.

ANDREW WIGET — Professor Emeritus of English at New Mexico State University. He spent two decades working with American Indians, and more recently has spent more than two decades working with Olga Balalaeva among the indigenous peoples of Siberia.

NATHAN ROMERO [Cochiti Pueblo] — Student at the Institute of American Indian Arts, Santa Fe, New Mexico. He studies creative writing and art, and assists in teaching and developing curricular materials for the Cochiti Keres Language Program.

JAMES WALTER — Professor of German at Ohio Northern University. He assisted with translations for *The Way of Kinship* and *MEDITATIONS After the Bear Feast*.

Shanti Arts

Art Nature Spirit

Shanti Arts celebrates art, nature, and spirit through exhibitions, publications, and workshops. For a complete list of our book and serial publications, along with information about exhibitions, submissions, artist opportunities, and educational events, please visit us online at www.shantiarts.com.

If you enjoyed this book and would like to purchase another copy, please visit your favorite bookstore, online bookseller, or contact the publisher directly. Online orders are accepted.

Shanti Arts
www.shantiarts.com
207-837-5760

Lightning Source UK Ltd.
Milton Keynes UK
UKOW07f1512110816

280481UK00014B/66/P